Table of Contents

Introduction

Most people can follow a high-protein diet by eating meat, fish, dairy products, beans and legumes, eggs, and vegetables that are relatively rich in protein, such as asparagus and spinach. People on this diet will often choose to reduce their carbohydrate intake, which may involve limiting their consumption of highly processed foods, bread and other baked goods, candy, and white pasta and rice. There are some well-known high-protein diet plans, such as the Atkins diet. However, a person can increase their protein intake on their own with or without adjusting their intake of other food groups. In this book, we explain how to eat a high-protein diet, foods to include and exclude, and the potential adverse effects of adopting this diet.

Benefits

• Protein is essential for building muscle.

• Unlike carbohydrates, protein provides long-lasting energy without an insulin surge (which promotes fat storage).

• Protein tends to suppress the appetite.

• Protein takes quite a bit of energy to digest, which boosts the body's metabolism.

• Lean protein-rich foods are much less calorie-dense than carbohydrate-rich foods. For example, the ham in a common sandwich may have 343 kJ per 100g, whereas the bread has 1011 kJ per 100g. Like vegetables, they help to bulk out a meal.

Risks

A person should speak to their doctor when considering a high-protein diet.

Most people can safely follow a high-protein diet, at least for a short period.

While some studies indicate that high levels of protein may negatively affect the kidneys, other research shows that people with healthy kidneys will not experience any adverse effects. However, clinical evidence does suggest that people with kidney disease should not eat a high-protein diet. Similarly, it seems that people who are susceptible to kidney stones should avoid high-protein diets, particularly those that include lots of animal proteins. People with other medical conditions should speak to a healthcare professional before adopting a high-protein diet. Although short-term studies show that high-protein diets can encourage weight loss, it is important to remember that there is no research looking at the long-term effects of high-protein diets on overall health.

Combining beans and legumes with other sources of protein can ensure a person gets all essential amino acids.

Choosing the right foods when eating a high-protein diet is important for maximum effectiveness.

Below are some excellent protein choices that could be suitable for a variety of dietary plans:

• Eggs

• Leaner cuts of beef

• Chicken breasts

• Turkey breasts

• Beans, such as garbanzo beans or black beans

• Shrimp

• Nuts and seeds, such as pumpkin seeds, peanuts, and almonds

• Fish, including salmon, flounder, and haddock

• Sprouted grain bread, such as ezekiel bread

• Whey or plant protein shakes

• Lentils

• Quinoa

• Chickpeas

• Oats

• Dairy products, such as greek yogurt, cow's milk, or cheese

• Vegetables, including Brussels sprouts and broccoli

People with necessary dietary restrictions should also continue to exclude unsuitable foods. For example, a person who has lactose intolerance should not use milk products to increase their protein intake.

A person should generally also avoid the following foods as part of the high-protein diet:

• Products that contain refined sugar, such as candy, baked goods, and sodas

• Highly processed foods

• Foods that manufacturers market as "diet" products, as they often contain excessive amounts of artificial sweetener

How To Eat A High-Protein Diet

Keeping a food journal can help when following a diet plan.

There are many possible ways to include more protein in the diet, even for those with other dietary restrictions.

For example, people who follow a vegetarian or vegan diet or those who avoid dairy can still eat a high-protein diet. People can either adjust their current diet to include more protein or follow a specific high-protein diet plan.

Taking the steps below may help a person when they start a high-protein diet:

• Figuring out their individual protein needs, which will depend on their body weight

• Making meal plans for the week

• Finding and using high-quality proteins

• Including at least 25–30 grams (g) of protein in each meal

• Keeping a food journal to track the amount and types of food that they eat

• Eating well-balanced meals

including both plant and lean animal sources of protein in the diet

High protein foods
Black beans

Black beans are often an inexpensive source of protein. Black beans can be prepared in a variety of ways, making them a very versatile ingredient when preparing meals.

Lima beans

Some Lima beans offer about 21 grams (g) of protein per 100 g serving.

Corn

Yellow corn has about 15.6 g of protein per cup. Additionally, corn also contains a good amount of fiber and minerals, including calcium.

Salmon

Salmon is considered a fatty fish, meaning it is full of omega-3 fatty acids. Salmon is also an excellent source of protein and can help a person feel more satisfied at meals. Salmon may not be as budget-friendly as some other protein options.

Potatoes

Potatoes have a reputation as a starchy carb but are good sources of nutrients, including protein. One medium potato with the skin on contains just over 4 g of protein. People should use caution when preparing a potato as the extras that people often put on potatoes can increase the calorie count.

Broccoli

One cup of raw broccoli has almost 2.6 g of protein and contains a variety of nutrients such as folate and potassium. This powerhouse veggie only has 31 calories per cup.

Cauliflower

Cauliflower has a lot of protein with very few calories. One cup of chopped cauliflower has 27 calories and 2 g of protein.

Chinese cabbage

Also known as bok choy, this vegetable gets much of its calories from protein and is full of antioxidants.

Eggs

Eggs are an excellent source of protein, nutrients, and healthful fats. A variety of studies have shown that eggs can help people feel more satisfied and stop them overeating. For example, one study found that a group of women who ate eggs instead of bagels for breakfast felt fuller for longer and ate fewer calories throughout the day.

Beef

Beef offers high amounts of protein per serving. There is a range of different types of beef to choose from for weight loss. People following a moderate carbohydrate diet should eat lean beef whereas a person on a low-carb diet may eat fattier beef.

Chicken breast

Chicken breast is a lean source of protein. The majority of its calories come directly from protein when served without skin. A 136 g skinless chicken breast provides around 26 g of protein.

Oats

Oats offer about 17 g of protein per 100g. They are also a source of complex carbohydrates. Raw oats are easy to prepare as oatmeal and people can flavor them with a variety healthful foods, such as fruits and nuts. People should avoid prepared oatmeals as they often contain added sugar.

Tuna

Tuna is an excellent and widely available source of protein that also has a low calorie count. Tuna is a lean fish with minimal fat. Add tuna to salads, sandwiches, and snacks. Be careful with additional dressings, such as mayonnaise, as these can add additional, unwanted calories.

Tempeh

Tempeh is a popular source of protein for vegetarians and vegans.

Tempeh comes from soybeans, like tofu. However, it has a higher protein count than tofu, offering about 17 g per half cup. Tempeh may not be easy to find, but some grocery stores carry it in the refrigerated vegetarian section.

Spirulina

Spirulina is a bacteria that grows in both fresh and salt waters. It offers a variety of nutrients and protein from a small amount of its powdered form.

Legumes

Legumes are both high in fiber and protein. This makes them a good choice as part of a weight loss diet because they can be quite filling. Some people may have trouble digesting legumes, however.

Hemp seeds

People can use hemp seeds in salads as a substitute for croutons. Hemp seeds offer about 9.5 g of protein per tablespoon. They are fairly easy to find in most grocery stores but can be expensive.

Sun-dried tomatoes

Sun-dried tomatoes are an excellent addition to many dishes and are widely available. They offer both a good source of protein, as well as additional nutrients and fiber.

Guava

Guava is a tropical fruit that may not be available everywhere. Guava is one of the most protein-rich fruits available. It also offers additional nutrients, such as vitamin C.

Artichokes

Artichokes are high in fiber and offer a good amount of protein. Artichokes are very versatile and are suitable for use in a variety of recipes. Artichokes are typically easy to find in most grocery stores.

Peas

Peas are high in protein, fiber, and other nutrients. Peas are inexpensive, easy to find, and can be used in lots of recipes.

Bison

Bison meat is another excellent source of protein. Bison is lean meat, offering less fat per serving than beef. Bison is becoming more available, and some people use it as a substitute for beef.

Pork

Lean pork is a good source of protein. Pork roasts and tenderloin are good choices for meals. People should avoid processed pork products such as bacon.

Turkey

Turkey packs a powerful punch of protein. Boneless turkey can provide about 13 g of protein per 100 g.

Chickpeas

Chickpeas are a healthful vegetarian protein that is high in fiber, and full of nutrients that support heart and bone health. They also ward off cancer.

Quinoa

Quinoa is one of the only complete sources of vegetarian protein. Quinoa contains all 11 amino acids needed to make a protein complete, making it an excellent choice for vegetarians, vegans, and those who do not eat a lot of meat.

Greek yogurt

Plain, low-fat Greek yogurt packs as much as 19 g of protein in a 200g pot. People looking to lose weight should limit or avoid Greek yogurt that contains added sugar. People should opt for the plain versions instead and jazz it up with some fruit or seeds.

Cottage cheese

This dairy product has an abundance of protein. It also offers a healthful serving of calcium and other nutrients.

Almonds

Nuts have a reputation for being high calorie but with a little bit of portion control, dry roasted or raw almonds can make for a filling, protein-rich snack.

Milk

Cow's milk is an excellent source of protein for people that can tolerate drinking milk. An 8 ounce serving of milk contains 8 g of protein.

Lentils

Lentils pack a hefty dose of plant protein and fiber. They are very affordable and may promote heart health.

Pumpkin seeds

Pumpkin seeds are full of protein and minerals, such as magnesium and selenium. People looking to lose weight should stay away from oil roasted pumpkin seeds and choose dry roasted seeds, instead.

Avocado

Avocados contain healthy fats, as well as protein.

Avocados not only contain protein and heart healthful unsaturated fat, but they also contain good levels of fiber and nutrients, such as potassium.

Portion control is necessary, however, since avocados are very calorie dense.

Pistachios

Pistachios are a reasonably low calorie nut that contain a big serving of protein.

One ounce of pistachios contains about 6 g of protein and a wealth of other nutrients including a high dose of B-6.

Chia seeds

This tiny seed packs more than 5 g of protein per ounce, along with omega-3s, fiber, and calcium. Vegans often use chia seeds as an egg substitute, and many people enjoy adding them to smoothies or salads for extra health benefits.

Nut butters

Nut butters, including peanut butter, contain a lot of calories, but a portion-controlled serving can add unsaturated fat and a dose of protein to a person's diet. People wanting to eat nut butters healthily should stick to those with no added sugars or oils.

Halibut

This white fish is an excellent source of lean protein with nearly 30 g of protein in half a fillet.

Asparagus

Asparagus gets over one quarter of its calories from protein. It is also full of nutrients, including B vitamins and is low in carbohydrates.

Watercress

This cruciferous vegetable grows in water, has a surprisingly high protein content, and contains a full day's worth of vitamin K. Adding some watercress to salads can really maximize its health benefits.

Brussel sprouts

Brussel sprouts are full of protein, fiber, and vitamins. A one cup serving contains almost 3 g of protein.

Spelt

Spelt is a type of hulled wheat that has a very high protein content. It has risen in popularity and is often available with the specialty flours.

Teff

Teff is a grass that is often ground down to make flour. This gluten-free food has a fairly high protein content with about 13 g of protein per 100 g serving.

Whey protein powder

Whey protein powder is used by many bodybuilders and athletes as a supplement to help increase muscle mass and strength. This powder is made from the proteins found in the liquid part of milk and can add a substantial amount of protein to a person's diet.

How to Follow a High-Protein Diet

The general rule that I like to follow for consuming protein is eating 50 percent of your body weight in grams of protein per day. Like I said, that means if you weigh 160 pounds, you should be consuming about 80 grams of protein per day. If you're looking to burn fat on a high-protein diet, then you'll want to consume even more protein, about 70 percent of your body weight. For people weighing 160 pounds, multiply 160 by 0.7, which gives you 112, so consume close to 100 to 115 grams of protein every day to burn fat more easily. An easy way to wrap your head around consuming enough protein in one day is to divide the amount of grams you want to eat by the number of meals you consume. If you eat three meals every day and you want to consume 80 grams of protein, then that's about 25 grams of protein per meal. Now break that down even further — 25 grams of protein is about a three-ounce serving (about the size of a deck of cards) of grass-fed beef, organic chicken or wild-caught salmon. Combine your meat with a serving of beans and you have plenty of protein in your meal already. Even leafy greens or vegetables like broccoli and Brussels sprouts contain some protein, so adding these vegetables and raw cheese to an omelette is another great way to consume over 25 grams of protein per meal. And to address your mid-day hunger, there are plenty of high-protein snacks that you can turn to. Examples of protein-rich snacks include black bean hummus, yogurt bites, deviled eggs and even cashew butter chocolate chip cookies. Which fruit has the most protein? Fruit is generally very low in protein, but if you eat a decent amount of fruit it can add up. Some of the best options for obtaining protein include guavas, avocados, apricots, kiwifruit, blackberries, oranges, bananas, cantaloupe, raspberries and peaches.

Meal Plan

Day 1

Breakfast (407 calories, 33 g protein)

• 1 serving Broccoli & Parmesan Cheese Omelet

• A.M. Snack (30 calories, 0 g protein)

• 1 medium plum

Lunch (402 calories, 16 g protein)

• 1 serving Butternut Squash Soup with Avocado & Chickpeas

• P.M. Snack (42 calories, 1 g protein)

• 1 kiwi

Dinner (319 calories, 26 g protein)

• 1 serving Citrus Poached Salmon with Asparagus

• 1/2 cup Easy Brown Rice

• Meal-Prep Tip: Consider making a double batch of Easy Brown Rice so you'll have enough to have for dinner on Day 2. Freeze any leftovers for up to 6 months.

Daily Totals: 1,200 calories, 77 g protein, 135 g carbohydrates, 22 g fiber, 41 g fat, 1,598 mg sodium

Day 2

veggies and rice in bowls with a side of fresh spinach

Breakfast (194 calories, 18 g protein)

• 1 cup raspberries

• 2/3 cup nonfat plain Greek yogurt

• 1 Tbsp. sliced almonds

• Top raspberries with yogurt and almonds.

• A.M. Snack (45 calories, 1 g protein)

• 1 kiwi

Lunch (519 calories, 34 g protein)

• 1 serving Mediterranean Chicken Quinoa Bowl

• Dinner (471 calories, 11 g protein)

• 1 serving Vegan Coconut Chickpea Curry

Daily Totals: 1,228 calories, 64 g protein, 130 g carbohydrates, 27 g fiber, 50 g fat, 1,315 mg sodium

Day 3

Plate of delicious-looking high-protein meal

Breakfast (239 calories, 26 g protein)

• 1 cup raspberries

• 1 cup nonfat plain Greek yogurt

• 1 Tbsp. sliced almonds

• Top raspberries with yogurt and almonds.

• 1 cup raspberries

Lunch (519 calories, 34 g protein)

• 1 serving Mediterranean Chicken Quinoa Bowl

P.M. Snack (42 calories, 1 g protein)

1 kiwi

Dinner (348 calories, 24 g protein)

• 1 serving Asian Beef Noodle Bowl

Daily Totals: 1,212 calories, 87 g protein, 112 g carbohydrates, 27 g fiber, 47 g fat, 1,265 mg sodium

Day 4

Breakfast (230 calories, 11 g protein)

• 1 serving Egg Salad Avocado Toast

• 1 cup raspberries

Lunch (519 calories, 34 g protein)

• 1 serving Mediterranean Chicken Quinoa Bowl

1 medium orange

Dinner (351 calories, 33 g protein)

• 1 serving Spicy Jerk Shrimp

Daily Totals: 1,225 calories, 81 g protein, 116 g carbohydrates, 26 g fiber, 50 g fat, 1,502 mg sodium

Day 5

Breakfast (230 calories, 11 g protein)

• 1 serving Egg Salad Avocado Toast

• 2 kiwis

Lunch (519 calories, 34 g protein)

• 1 serving Mediterranean Chicken Quinoa Bowl

• 1 cup raspberries

Dinner (318 calories, 26 g protein)

• 1 serving Zucchini Parmesan

Daily Totals: 1,215 calories, 74 g protein, 106 g carbohydrates, 27 g fiber, 58 g fat, 1,740 mg sodium

Day 6

Garlic-Lime Pork with Farro & Spinach

Breakfast (272 calories, 27 g protein)

- 1 cup raspberries

- 1 cup nonfat plain Greek yogurt

- 1 Tbsp. sliced almonds

- Top raspberries with yogurt and almonds.

- 1 kiwi

Lunch (387 calories, 14 g protein)

- 1 serving Veggie & Hummus Sandwich

- 1 medium orange

- 1 cups edamame (in pods), sprinkled with coarse sea salt to taste

Dinner (416 calories, 41 g protein)

- 1 serving Garlic-Lime Pork with Farro & Spinach

- 2 servings Tangy Broccoli with Almonds

Daily Totals: 1,217 calories, 90 g protein, 136 g carbohydrates, 39 g fiber, 39 g fat, 1,278 mg sodium

Day 7

Salmon Tacos with Pineapple Salsa

Breakfast (212 calories, 8 g protein)

• 1 servingTwo-Ingredient Banana Pancakes

• 1/2 cup raspberries

• 1 Tbsp. maple syrup

• 1/2 cup nonfat plain Greek yogurt with 1 plum, chopped

Lunch (325 calories, 18 g protein)

• 1 serving Green Salad with Edamame & Beets

• 1 slice whole-wheat bread, toasted

• 1/4 avocado, mashed

Top toast with avocado and season with a pinch each of salt, pepper and crushed red pepper.

Dinner (422 calories, 27 calories)

• 1 serving Salmon Tacos with Pineapple Salsa

• 1 serving Broiled Mango to enjoy after dinner

Daily Totals: 1,208 calories, 70 g protein, 144 g carbohydrates, 30 g fiber, 41 g fat, 1,743 mg sodium.

Easy, Gluten-Free Beef Stroganoff
INGREDIENTS:

• 1 package gluten-free egg noodles

• 1 pound grass-fed ground beef

• ¼ cup Worcestershire sauce

• 1½ cup mushrooms, chopped

• ½ cup plain, grass-fed goat or sheep yogurt

• 1 tablespoon garlic powder

• 1 tablespoon onion powder

• 2 teaspoons sea salt or Himalayan pink salt

• 2 teaspoons pepper

• 1 tablespoon arrowroot starch

• ¼ cup water

INSTRUCTIONS:

• Cook egg noodles according to package instructions.

• In a large skillet, over medium-high heat, add in ground beef.

• Using a wooden spoon, break up ground beef into equal pieces and cook for 5 minutes, or until beef is almost done.

• Add in Worcestershire sauce and mushrooms and cook for an additional 10 minutes.

• Reduce heat to medium-low.

• Add in remaining ingredients, except the noodles and water and simmer for 10–12 minutes.

• Slowly add in water until desired thickness is reached.

• Add in the noodles, stirring until well-combined.

• Add salt and pepper to taste.

• Top with additional parsley if desired.

INGREDIENTS:

• 12-14 ounces canned wild caught salmon

• 3 minced garlic cloves

• 2 tablespoons minced green onions

• 2 tablespoons chopped fresh cilantro

• 3 eggs

• 2 tablespoons lime juice

• 1 tablespoon mustard

• ½ teaspoon black pepper

• 1 teaspoon sea salt

• ¼ cup coconut flour

• Coconut oil for greasing pan

INSTRUCTIONS:

• In a bowl, mix the salmon, garlic, green onions and cilantro.

• In a separate bowl, combine the eggs, lime juice, mustard, pepper and salt.

• Combine both mixtures until well incorporated.

• Add in coconut flour and mix again.

• Form four patties.

• In a greased pan over medium high heat, add patties.

• Cook burgers until browned or reaches an internal temperature of 145 F and then flip (about 4 minutes each side).

Turmeric Eggs Recipe

INGREDIENTS:

• 4 eggs

• 2 ounces raw goat or sheep cheese, shredded

• 3 tablespoons ghee

• ½ cup red onions, chopped

• 8 green onions, chopped

• 1 cup yellow peppers, chopped

- 6 cloves of garlic, minced

- 1 tablespoon thyme

- 1 tablespoon oregano

- 1 tablespoon basil

- 2 tablespoons turmeric

INSTRUCTIONS:

- Sauté onions, green onions and garlic in pan with ghee over medium-low heat for 10 minutes.

- Add in eggs, cheese and herbs.

- Cook for 10 minutes, stirring continuously and add in turmeric.

Classic Hummus Recipe

INGREDIENTS

- 2 cups garbanzo beans, drained and rinsed

- 2 cloves garlic, minced

- ⅓ cup tahini

- ¼ cup lemon juice

- 1 teaspoon sea salt

- 1 tablespoon olive oil

- paprika to taste

INSTRUCTIONS

- Drain and rinse the garbanzo beans.

- Mince two cloves of garlic.

- Place all ingredients (except for the paprika) into a food processor and blend until smooth.

- Scrap hummus out of food processor container and place into a small dish or storage container. Sprinkle paprika on top.

Keto Smoothie Recipe with Avocado, Chia Seeds & Cacao

INGREDIENTS:

- 1–1¼ cups full-fat coconut milk

- ½ frozen avocado

• 1 tablespoon nut butter of choice

• 1 tablespoon chia seeds, soaked in 3 tablespoons of water for 10 minutes

• 2 teaspoons cacao nibs, cacao powder or cocoa powder OR 1 scoop of chocolate protein powder made from bone broth

• 1 tablespoon coconut oil

ice (optional*)

• for topping: cacao nibs and cinnamon

• ¼ cup water, if needed

INSTRUCTIONS:

• Add contents into a high-powered blender, blending until well-combined.

• Top with cacao nibs and cinnamon.

High Protein Chicken Salad

High Protein Chicken Salad! Made with Greek yogurt, grapes & bell peppers this recipe is healthy, easy mayo free

& egg free. Great for a quick meal, light lunch or appetizer. Low Carb + Gluten Free + Low Calorie

High Protein Chicken Salad! Made with Greek yogurt, grapes & bell peppers this recipe is healthy, easy mayo free & egg free. Great for a quick meal, light lunch or appetizer. Gluten Free + Low Calorie

Ingredients

• 12 ounces chicken breast canned in water

• 1/2 cup Greek yogurt

• 1/2 cup green bell pepper diced

• 1/2 cup red grapes sliced in half

• 1/2 tsp sage

• 1 tsp thyme

• 1 tbsp lemon juice

Instructions

• Drain the water from the chicken then add all the ingredients to a bowl to combine.

• Divide the mixture into fours then place in meal prep containers.

Ingredients

• 28 ounces tofu blocks, extra-firm, organic

• 3 pounds yukon gold potatoes

• 1 onion medium, roughly chopped

• 8 ounces mushrooms package, sliced

• 2 carrots large, or 3 medium

• 1/2 cup green beans fresh or frozen

• 10 ounces peas package, frozen

• 1/2 cup sweet corn kernels fresh or frozen

• 2 tablespoons Italian seasoning or equal blend of basil, marjoram, oregano, rosemary and thyme

• 1 tablespoon dried oregano

• 3 Not-Chick'n Cubes

• 1 tablespoon arrowroot powder or cornstarch

• salt and black pepper to taste

• 1 1/2 cups vegetable broth or as needed

Instructions

• Press water out of tofu blocks using a tofu press or alternative method, then slice blocks sideways and lengthwise into 4-5 planks, and then cut planks into 1/2" cubes.

• Boil whole potatoes or steam until soft and easily pierced with a fork. Drain water and mash potatoes thoroughly by hand, or using a mixer, until smooth and all lumps are removed, adding vegetable broth as needed. The mashed potatoes should be able to spread easily over the pie. Cover and set aside.

• Preheat oven to 350.

• Add 1/3 cup vegetable broth to a non-stick sauté pan, then sauté onions and mushrooms over medium-high heat until onions are semi-translucent, replenishing vegetable broth and deglazing pan as needed.

• Add salt, pepper, and seasonings. Add remainder of vegetables and sauté for about 5 minutes, or until al dente. When finished, add cooked vegetables to the deep dish pan.

• Add 1/2 cup of vegetable broth to the same non-stick pan over medium-high heat until bubbling. Add tofu cubes and sauté until browned, replenishing vegetable broth and deglazing pan as the broth evaporates.

• When browned, add tofu cubes and toss with the cooked vegetables.

• Add 4 cups water to the same non-stick sauté pan, then add 3 Not-Chick'n Cubes to water, add arrowroot powder or cornstarch, and bring to a boil for 5 minutes to reduce a bit. Add this broth to the deep dish pan.

• Add additional salt and pepper to taste. Spread mashed potatoes evenly over the vegetable broth mixture. Mashed potato layer should be at least 1-inch thick.

• Bake mixture uncovered for one hour.

• If desired, set oven to broil or increase oven temperature to 450 degrees for 10 minutes to crisp the top of the mashed potatoes.

Nutrition Information

Serving: 1.25cups | Calories: 278kcal | Carbohydrates: 39g |
Protein: 18g | Fat: 7g | Saturated Fat: 1g | Sodium: 788mg |
Fiber: 8g | Sugar: 5g | SmartPoints (Freestyle): 3

Keto Cauliflower Fried Rice Recipe, Low Calorie, Low Carb

INGREDIENTS

- 2 tbsp sesame oil — or olive oil, divided

- 2 eggs — large, beaten

- 1/4 cup diced onion

- 2 cloves garlic

- 1/2 cup peas — frozen would work

- 1/2 cup carrots — can use more if you'd like

- 1 medium head of cauliflower

- 3 scallions — green part only

- 3 tbsp soy sauce or Tamari

- 1 tsp sesame seeds

INSTRUCTIONS

• Cut cauliflower into florets. Wash and dry. Place in a food processor (work in batches) and pulse 6-7 times, until the cauliflower gets the texture of couscous. Don't leave the pieces too big and don't over process.

• Heat 1 tbsp of the oil in a large skillet over medium heat. Add the beaten eggs, let them cook for 1 minute, then scramble, cook for 1-2 more minutes, then remove and transfer to a plate.

• Add the remaining oil to the skillet. Add the onion and garlic, cook for 2 minutes, stirring frequently, being careful not to burn them. Add the carrot and peas, cook for for 2-3 more minutes.

• Add the cauliflower. Turn the heat to medium-high and cook for 5 more minutes, stirring frequently. Add the soy sauce. Add the eggs. Cook for 1 more minute, then transfer to a bowl. Top with scallions and sesame seeds (optional)

NUTRITION INFORMATION

Calories: 84, Fat: 6g, Saturated Fat: 1g, Cholesterol: 54mg, Sodium: 30mg, Potassium: 110mg, Carbohydrates: 4g,

Fiber: 1g, Sugar: 1g, Protein: 2g, Vitamin A: 2015%, Vitamin C: 7.4%, Calcium: 24%, Iron: 0.6%

Cauliflower Rice Chicken Enchilada Casserole

Ingredients

• 12 oz package of Mann's Riced Cauliflower (340 g)

• 1 cup corn kernels

• 2 cans enchilada sauce 20 oz, roughly 2.5 cups

• 2 cups cooked rotisserie chicken chopped

• Four 6 inch flour tortillas cut in half

• 1 1/2 cups mozzarella cheese or Monterey jack, shredded

Garnishes

• Avocado

• Fresh tomatoes

• Cilantro

Instructions

• Heat oven to 350°F.

• Microwave the riced cauliflower (in the sealed package) for 2 minutes. Allow to cool slightly before opening the bag and adding to a large bowl.

• Stir in the corn, enchilada sauce, chicken, and ½ cup cheese (optional).

• In the bottom of a 9x9 inch baking dish, place four of the tortillas, flat side to the outside of the container.

• Top with the filling.

• Add two more tortillas on top, then sprinkle with 1 cup of cheese.

• Bake for 30 minutes.

• Serve with avocado, tomatoes and greek yogurt (or sour cream)

Notes

Mann's Culinary Cuts Cauliflower Cauliettes can be found:

Ontario – Sobey's, IGA, Metro, Longo'sBC – Nestor's, Save On Foods, Sobey's, SafewayAlberta – Save On

Foods, Sobey's and SafewayQuebec – Metro, IGA, Sobey's

Nutrition

Serving: 1/9 batch | Calories: 189kcal | Carbohydrates: 17g | Protein: 16g | Fat: 6g | Saturated Fat: 1g | Cholesterol: 29mg | Sodium: 729mg | Fiber: 3g | Sugar: 3g

Spiralized Pad Thai Chicken Meal Prep Bowls

These Spiralized Pad Thai Chicken Meal Prep Bowls are a healthier, low-carb version of Thai takeout with spiralized zucchini, matchstick carrots, red cabbage and an easy Pad Thai sauce!

Ingredients

• 1 tbsp olive or coconut oil

• 1 small yellow onion, diced

• 4 chicken breasts

• 4 zucchinis, spiralized or cut into matchsticks

• 1 package Carrot matchsticks

• 1/2 red cabbage, thinly chopped

- 2-3 scallions, sliced

- 1/4 cup chopped peanuts

- 1/3 cup finely chopped cilantro

- Pad Thai Sauce

- 1/4 cup tamarind paste

- 1 tbsp low-sodium soy sauce or tamari

- 1 tbsp peanut butter

- 2 cloves garlic minced

- 2 tsp fish sauce

- 2 tsp lime juice

Instructions

- Whisk ingredients for Pad Thai sauce together in a medium-sized glass bowl.

- Heat olive oil on med-high heat. Add onions, sauteeing for 2-3 min until softened. Add chicken and 3/4 of the Pad Thai Sauce, stirring to combine and cooking for 8-10 min until chicken is fully cooked.

• Remove from heat and add zucchini noodles, sauteeing for 30 seconds with remaining Pad Thai sauce. Remove from heat immediately and add to glass meal prep bowls (I got mine from IKEA!)

• Add chicken, carrots and red cabbage to each bowl, garnishing with scallions, peanuts and cilantro. Refrigerate up to 4-5 days and take for work!

Nutrition

Calories: 382kcal | Carbohydrates: 26g | Protein: 30g | Fat: 19g | Saturated Fat: 3g | Polyunsaturated Fat: 2g | Monounsaturated Fat: 6g | Cholesterol: 62mg | Sodium: 532mg | Potassium: 751mg | Fiber: 6g | Sugar: 14g | Vitamin A: 1050IU | Vitamin C: 66.8mg | Calcium: 80mg | Iron: 2.3mg

Peanut Butter Protein Balls

These yummy low-carb Peanut Butter Protein Balls are among my favorite healthy snacks! They are easy to make, no-bake, gluten-free, and will stay fresh in the fridge for days.

Ingredients

- 1 cup creamy unsalted peanut butter

- 1½ scoop vanilla protein powder

- ½ tsp. vanilla extract

- 1 tsp. cinnamon

- 2 tsp. Stevia

- 20 raw, unsalted peanuts

Instructions

- Mix together all ingredients except the raw peanuts in a bowl until smooth.

- Roll the dough into 1 or 1½ inch balls. You should end up with 15.

- Place the raw peanuts in a blender (I use my NutriBullet) and pulse several times until you have small pieces. If you don't have a blender, you can chop them instead.

- Roll the balls in the peanut crumbles and transfer them to a baking sheet lined with parchment paper.

• Place in the refrigerator and let set for at least 20-30 minutes.

Sheet Pan Greek Chicken Meal Prep Bowls

These Sheet Pan Greek Chicken Meal Prep Bowls are a low carb make ahead lunch idea seasoned with a simple lemon-oregano marinade, and they're ready in just 30 minutes!

Ingredients

• 1 lb chicken breasts, diced

• 1 red pepper, diced

• 1 yellow pepper, diced

• 1 zucchini, thickly sliced

• 1 red onion, thickly sliced

• 2 tbsp olive oil

• 2 tbsp lemon juice

• 4 cloves garlic minced

• 1 tbsp oregano

• 1 tsp salt

• 1/2 tsp pepper

• 1/4 cup feta cheese, crumbled (leave out for Whole 30)

Instructions

• Preheat oven to 400 F. Add all ingredients except for feta to a large sheet pan and toss well to combine. Bake in oven once preheated for 18-20 minutes until chicken is fully cooked.

• Remove from oven and divide mixture among 4 glass meal prep bowls. Top with feta cheese (optional) and serve. Keeps in fridge up to 5 days.

Egg Muffins Recipe

Ingredients

Egg Cups with Mushrooms, Spinach, and Cheese are the perfect high-protein meal or snack to have on hand in the fridge.

• 1 tablespoon olive oil

• 8 ounces white button mushrooms sliced

• Salt and freshly ground black pepper

• 10 ounces fresh spinach leaves + ¼ cup water OR 10 ounces frozen spinach, thawed

• 6 eggs lightly beaten

• 6 ounces feta cheese crumbled

Instructions

• Preheat oven to 375°F. Coat a muffin tin with nonstick cooking spray.

• To sauté the mushrooms (optional, see notes):

• In a large skillet over medium-high heat, heat oil until shimmering. Add mushrooms and ¼ teaspoon salt and cook until softened and the mushrooms have released most of their liquid, about 5 minutes.

• Using a slotted spoon, remove mushrooms from skillet to a large mixing bowl, leaving any remaining oil and liquid in the skillet.

To use fresh spinach:

• Add to the skillet with water and sauté until tender and wilted, about 10 minutes. Drain and place in a clean kitchen towel. Squeeze and twist the towel to remove as much liquid as possible.

To use frozen spinach (thawed):

• Sauté in pan until heated through, about 5 minutes. Drain and place in a clean kitchen towel. Squeeze and twist the towel to remove as much liquid as possible.

To make the egg muffins:

• Add the spinach to the bowl with the mushrooms. Stir in eggs, cheese, ½ teaspoon salt, and ¼ teaspoon pepper.

• Divide egg mixture evenly among 12 muffin cups. Bake until a toothpick inserted comes out clean, about 25 minutes.

• Cool slightly before removing from muffin tins (the egg cups should come out easily). Serve hot or at room temperature. Store leftovers in the refrigerator and use within 4 days.

To freeze the muffins:

• Cool and transfer to a single layer on a plate. Freeze until solid, at least 30 minutes, then transfer to a freezer-safe bag. Freeze up to 2 months.

To reheat the muffins:

• Microwave them straight from the freezer until heated through, about 1 minute.

Broccoli Cauliflower Rice Chicken Casserole

This low carb and cheesy Broccoli Cauliflower Rice Chicken Casserole recipe is perfect for dinner and makes great leftovers. It's also gluten free!

INGREDIENTS

• 2 pounds skinless boneless chicken breasts

• 1 tablespoon olive oil

• 2 10-ounce bags frozen cauliflower rice (or 1 head of cauliflower, riced and cooked)

• 1 16-ounce bag frozen broccoli cuts

• 2 large eggs, whisked

• 3 cups, shredded mozzarella cheese

• 2 teaspoons coarse sea salt

• 2 teaspoons garlic powder

• 2 teaspoons onion powder

• 2 tablespoons butter, melted

• 1 cup shredded Italian blend cheese

INSTRUCTIONS

• Preheat oven to 400°F. Spray a large 3-quart baking dish with non-stick cooking spray or olive oil. Set aside.

• Slice chicken breasts in half horizontally to make them thinner, lightly coat them in olive oil and place on a baking sheet. Liberally season with salt and pepper and bake for 20 minutes.

• While the chicken is baking, heat the bags of frozen cauliflower rice and broccoli according to package instructions. Discard any excess water or moisture.

• Remove chicken from oven and let cool for 5 minutes. Carefully chop baked chicken into bite-sized pieces.

• In a large bowl, add cooked cauliflower rice, broccoli, chicken, eggs, mozzarella cheese, salt, garlic powder, onion powder and butter. Toss together until fully combined.

• Transfer casserole mixture to the prepared baking dish and top with the remaining Italian blend cheese.

• Bake for 50 minutes, until the cheese on top has fully melted and started to brown slightly. Let cool for 10 minutes before serving.

Meal Prep Protein Bowls (Gluten Free)

INGREDIENTS

• 4 cups mixed greens

• 4 hard boiled eggs, see below for Instant Pot recipe

• 2 cups shredded cooked chicken breast, see below for Instant Pot recipe

• 1 cup cooked red quinoa

• 1/2 large English cucumber, sliced

• 1/2 cup Homemade Ranch dressing, or dressing of choice

INSTRUCTIONS

• Divide all ingredients equally among 4 containers. Seal and refrigerate until ready to eat.

• Keep dressing separate until ready to serve and pour over bowl.

NUTRITION

calories: 249kcal, carbohydrates: 13g, protein: 25g, fat: 11g, saturated fat: 3g, cholesterol: 241mg, sodium: 272mg, potassium: 430mg, fiber: 1g, sugar: 2g, vitamin a: 777iu, vitamin c: 10mg, calcium: 53mg, iron: 2mg

High Protein Vegan "Meat"balls

Ingredients:

• 1 large brown onion, diced

• 400g (approximately 14 oz) of tinned brown lentils, drained

• 1 cup mushrooms, washed and finely sliced

• 1 tbsp extra virgin olive oil

• ½ cup quinoa, cooked

• 1 zucchini, grated

- ½ cup plain rolled oats

- 1 garlic clove, crushed

- 3 tbsp chia seeds

- 1 tbsp sweet chili sauce

- 9 tbsp water

- 1 small chili, finely chopped

Instructions:

- Preheat the oven to 175° C (350° F).

- Heat oil on pan. Add onion, garlic, chili and brown. Add mushrooms and lentils. Heat for a few minutes. Set aside.

- In a small bowl, mix chia and water. Set aside.

- In a large bowl, combine cooked lentils and onion mix, chia, quinoa, oats, zucchini and chili sauce. After that, mix until combined well.

- Roll into balls with hands and place on an oiled baking tray.

• Finally, bake for approximately 10 minutes or until golden brown.

• Serve and enjoy.

High Protein Satay Tempeh (gluten-free)

This high protein vegan meal is an excellent option for lunch or dinner. Made with tempeh, quinoa and nuts, it provides a great protein hit along with fiber, vitamins and minerals.

Ingredients:

For the Tofu and Veggies:

• 250g (approximately 9 oz) firm tofu, cubed

• 2 cups baby spinach, shredded

• 1 red onion, diced

• 1/2 cup pumpkin, diced

• 1 tbsp sesame seed oil

• 2 tbsp black sesame seeds

• Sprinkle of chili flakes

• 1 small lime, halved

• 1 cup of quinoa, cooked

For the Satay Sauce:

• 1/4 cup roasted, unsalted peanuts

• 1 tbsp sesame seed oil

• 1 lime, juiced

• 2 tbsp Tamari or soy sauce

Instructions:

• Steam pumpkin. Remove from heat and place in bowl.

• In a blender, combine satay ingredients. Remove and put aside.

• Next, heat sesame seed oil in a wok and cook onion until translucent. Remove from pan.

• Add tofu to pan and cook. Then, once cooked through, stir in satay sauce and coat.

• Remove tofu from pan and place in bowl with veggies. Sprinkle with sesame seeds, coconut & chili.

• Combine all ingredients and sprinkle with fresh lime juice.

• Serve and enjoy!

Vegetarian Black Bean Dip

Ingredients:

• 1 can black beans, drained

• 1 tsp fresh diced chili

• 2 cloves garlic, crushed

• 1 tbsp extra virgin olive oil

• 5 cm (1 inch) ginger, grated

• 1 small lime, juiced

Instructions:

• Heat oil on a frying pan and cook garlic, chili and ginger. Add beans and cook for a few more minutes.

• Remove from heat and place into a high-speed blender. Next, add lime juice and blitz until smooth and well combined.

• Serve with some wholegrain crackers or veggie sticks and enjoy!

Plant Protein Breakfast Smoothie

This breakfast smoothie is a quick and easy option that you can drink on the go to boost your protein intake in the mornings. Additionally, it can make an excellent post-workout snack.

Ingredients:

• 1 frozen banana

• 350ml (approximately 1 ½ cups) soy milk

• 2 tbsp hemp seeds

• ½ cup plain rolled oats

• 1 tbsp nut butter

• 1 tsp honey

Instructions:

• First, place all ingredients into a blender. Next, blend until smooth.

• Finally, pour into a cup. It's ready to enjoy!

Cucumber Tuna Boats

These high protein, low carb cucumber tuna boats will hit the spot!

Ingredients

• 1 medium cucumber about 100 grams

• 1 Pouch tuna fish, packed in water (70 calories)

• 1 tablespoon light mayonnaise

• 1 slice turkey bacon optional

• 3-4 small cherry tomatoes, Optional

Instructions

• Slice cucumber length wise, and scrape out the center seeds.

• Combine tuna with light mayonnaise

• Cook 1 slice of turkey bacon in the microwave, according to package directions (optional)

• Slice a cherry tomato into small slices (optional)

• Scoop tuna into the hollowed out cucumber.

• Top with chopped turkey bacon and sliced cherry tomatoes.

Nutrition

Serving: 1cucumber | Calories: 130kcal | Carbohydrates: 1g | Protein: 19g | Fat: 6g

The Sirtfood Diet Green Juice

Ingredients

• 75 g kale

• 30 g rocket

• 5 g parsley

• 2 celery sticks

• ½ green apple

• 1 cm ginger

• Juice of ½ lemon

• ½ teaspoon matcha green tea

Instructions

• Juice all the ingredients apart from the lemon and the matcha green tea.

• Squeeze the lemon juice into the green juice by hand.

• Pour a small amount of green juice into a glass and stir in the matcha. Add the rest of the green juice into the glass and stir again.

• Drink straight away or save for later.

Skinny Chicken Salad

Ingredients

• 4 ounces shredded or diced (cooked) boneless, skinless, chicken breast (abt 1 cup)

• 1/4 cup diced celery

• 2 tablespoons sliced green onion

• 1/4 cup diced sweet, crisp apple

• 1 tablespoon light mayo

• 1 tablespoon light sour cream or Greek yogurt

• optional: 1/2-1 Tablespoon chopped fresh parsley or cilantro

• 1/8 teaspoon curry powder

• 1/4 teaspoon red wine vinegar

• 1 tablespoon toasted sliced almonds

• salt and pepper to taste

Instructions

• Combine all ingredients except almonds and stir to combine. If possible, chill for an hour or so before eating.

• Before serving, mix in almonds.

• Eat in a lettuce wrap, on whole grain bread, in a wrap, or in a pita.

Cheesy beans for a High Protein vegetarian diet plan

INGREDIENTS

• Onions

• All purpose flour

• Veg oil

• Green beans (blanched)

• Paprika, garlic, salt

• Grated cheese of your choice

INSTRUCTIONS

• Start by preparing some crispy fried onions. You can make these by simply slicing some white onions and dust them with a little all-purpose flour before frying them on high in some oil until they are crispy and golden brown.

• Whilst frying in a baking dish, layout the blanched green beans and drizzle a lovely dollop of olive oil over them. Sprinkle with some chopped garlic (or garlic powder), paprika powder and salt, and pop them in the oven n too until crisp

• Top them with some grated cheese of any kind, a handful of the fried onions and bake again for a minute, and then tuck in.

Protein Rich Soy Dosa Recipe

Ingredients

• 1/4 cup Soy flour

- 1/4 cup White Urad Dal (Whole) , soaked overnight

- 3/4 cup Rice flour

- 1 cup Water , (divided)

- Salt

- Sunflower Oil , to smear on dosa

Instructions

- To begin making Protein Rich Soy Dosa Recipe, soak urad dal in water for about 4 hours or overnight. Drain the water completely from the dal and grind them into a fine paste with 1/4 cup of water.

- Combine urad dal, rice flour, and soya flour together in a large bowl.

- Add the 3/4 cup water to the flour and combine them together. The batter should be in the consistency of dosa batter. Adjust water if required.

- Season the batter with salt.

• Heat the dosa tawa. Once the tawa is hot, take a ladleful of batter and pour on the heated tawa. Spread it in a circular motion.

• Smear little oil on the dosa and along the edges of it.

• Cook until the dosa becomes brownish. Flip over the other side and cook until both the sides of dosa become light brownish.

• Repeat the same procedure for the remaining batter.

• Serve Protein Rich Soy Dosa Recipe with Karanataka Style Goraikai Kara Recipe or any chutney of your choice.

Banana Protein Bread

Ingredients

• 1/3 cup coconut oil, melted + additional for greasing

• 1 cup gluten-free all-purpose flour + additional for dusting

• 1 cup almond flour

• ½ cup protein powder (TRY: Garden of Life Raw Organic Protein Powder)

• ½ tsp sea salt

• 2 tsp baking powder

• 1 tsp ground cinnamon (TRY: Simply Organic Ground Cinnamon)

• ½ tsp baking soda

• ¼ tsp ground nutmeg (TRY: Simply Organic Ground Nutmeg)

• 3 bananas, mashed (about 1½ cups)

• 3 large eggs, room temperature

• ½ cup whole-milk Greek yogurt

• 1 tsp pure vanilla extract (TRY: Simply Organic Vanilla Extract)

Instruction

• Preheat oven to 375°F. Grease a 9 x 5-inch loaf pan with oil and dust with flour, tapping out excess.

• In a large bowl, whisk together all-purpose and almond flours, protein powder, salt, baking powder, cinnamon, baking soda and nutmeg.

• In a separate large bowl, whisk together bananas, oil, coconut sugar, eggs, yogurt and vanilla until smooth. Pour banana mixture into flour mixture. Stir well until dry ingredients are incorporated. Transfer to prepared pan.

• Bake for 50 minutes, or until a toothpick inserted into the center of the loaf comes out clean. Let cool in pan for 10 minutes then transfer loaf to a wire rack to cool completely. Cut into 10 slices. Store in an airtight container at room temperature for up to 3 days, or freeze for longer storage.

Sheet Pan Pesto Chicken Meal Prep Bowls

These Sheet Pan Pesto Chicken Meal Prep Bowls are a delicious way to enjoy your veggies and basil pesto, and they're a low carb lunch idea that comes together in 30 minutes!

Ingredients

• 2 tbsp olive oil, divided

• 1 cup basil, packed

- 1/4 cup Parmesan cheese

- 2 cloves garlic minced

- 1/2 tsp salt

- 1/2 tsp pepper

- 3 chicken breasts, diced

- 1 cup mushrooms cut in half

- 1 cup Cherry tomatoes

- 1 head broccoli, cut into florets

- 1 small zucchini, cut thickly

Instructions

- Preheat oven to 400 F. In a Magic Bullet, blender or food processor, blend 1 tbsp olive oil, basil, parmesan cheese, garlic, salt and pepper together until smooth (you may need to add 1-2 tsp of water to get it to blend).

- Add chicken and mushrooms to large sheet pan and toss with 1 tbsp of olive oil and 2 tbsp of pesto. Bake in oven for 10 minutes. Remove from oven and drain excess liquid.

• Add remaining vegetables and the rest of pesto. Toss to combine then bake another 10 minutes until chicken is fully cooked. Remove from oven and divide among 4 meal prep bowls. Keeps in fridge up to 5 days.